A New True Book

PREHISTORIC PEOPLE

By Ovid K. Wong, Ph. D.

CHILDRENS PRESS ®

CHICAGO

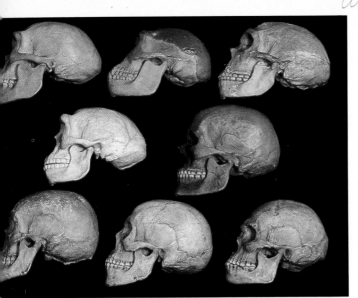

A display of prehistoric skulls

PHOTO CREDITS

AP/Wide World Photos, Inc.—18 (left), 35, 44 (top left)

© Bruce Coleman, Inc.—2, 6 (left), 13, 21, 28, 29, 30 (top & bottom right), 37, 38, 44 (bottom left)

Historical Pictures Service, Chicago—8

Image Finders: © R. Flanagan—42

Journalism Services:
© Mark Gamba—14
© SIU—6 (right)
© Susanne Suffredin—44 (top right)

© Norma Morrison—4 (bottom right), 7 (left)

Odyssey Productions: © Robert Frerck—cover, 7 (right), 18 (right), 25, 30 (left), 32, 41, 44 (middle and bottom right)

Root Resources:
© Wanda Christl—4 (bottom left)
© Ted Farrington—11, 17
© Kenneth Rapalee—23
© Mary Root—4 (top), 33

Horizon Graphics—map, 17, 26, 28

Cover: Diorama of Homo erectus at the Field Museum, Chicago

This book is dedicated to Mrs. H. C. L. Lee, my godmother, who is ever so loving and caring.

Library of Congress Cataloging-in-Publication Data

Wong, Ovid K.
  Prehistoric people / by Ovid K. Wong.
      p.   cm. — (A New true book)
  Includes index.
  Summary: Discusses the characteristics which make human beings different from other species and describes how scientists have learned about prehistoric people and their evolution.
  ISBN 0-516-01217-7
  1. Man, Prehistoric—Juvenile literature. 2. Fossil man—Juvenile literature. 3. Human evolution—Juvenile literature. [1. Man, Prehistoric. 2. Human evolution.] I. Title.
GN744.W66 1988   87-33781
573.3—dc19   CIP
                                          AC

TABLE OF CONTENTS

Humans can use their flexible thumbs
to hold a needle, open a door,
or turn a screwdriver.

WHAT ARE HUMANS?

What are humans? How do they differ from other animals? Scientists say three characteristics set humans apart from other animals.

Humans are good with their hands. Each human hand has a flexible thumb. The thumb lets humans grip things firmly. We can grip a big screwdriver or a tiny sewing needle. In comparison

 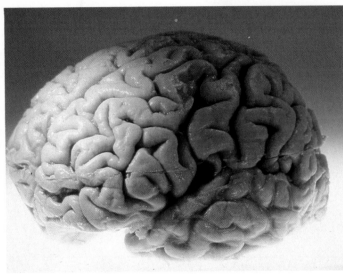

The chimpanzee (left) has a short thumb. Its brain is smaller than a human brain (right).

apes have shorter thumbs and
their hand grip is clumsy.

The human brain is
much larger and has more
brain cells than any other
animal. This gives humans
more brain power and
intelligence.

6

How does walking
upright help humans?
Walking upright leaves the
hands free to do other
work.

Skill with our hands,
intelligence, and walking
upright give humans an

7

Carolus Linnaeus
(1707-1778)

advantage over other
animals in the struggle for
survival.

In science all living
plants and animals,
including people, are put
into groups. In 1758 the
Swedish botanist Carolus

Linnaeus gave two Latin
names to all living things.
The first name describes a
big group, or genus. The
second name describes a
little group under the big
group, the species.

Scientists call humans of
today *Homo sapiens*.
Homo, the first name,
means "man." All people
who have ever lived

belong to this genus. *Sapiens*, the second name, means "wise" or "intelligent." The name, *Homo sapiens*, means "man the wise" or "intelligent man."

Most prehistoric people were not as developed as *Homo sapiens*. Therefore, they were given a different species name.

HOW SCIENTISTS STUDY PREHISTORIC PEOPLE

Before human beings
could write, they left only
their bones and the
remains of their shelters
and tools. These remains

Fossils uncovered at the Olduvai Gorge in Africa.

can give us some information. But they do not tell us which events happened when. The time before history was written down is called prehistoric, meaning before recorded history. The people who lived at that time are called prehistoric people.

Scientists look for the places where prehistoric people might have lived. They dig into the earth

Scientist
examines a skull
found in
Caesarea, Israel.

looking for objects or
bones left by these people.
Scientists carefully study
these objects and fossils
to find out how old they are.

13

Because of carbon dating scientists know these bodies were buried before the Incas ruled Peru.

The age of fossils can be found by a process called carbon dating. This method is based on the fact that radioactive carbon (carbon 14) is found in fixed amounts in the cells of all living plants and animals. When a plant or animal dies, the carbon 14 in the cells begin to break down, or decay. As a result, the amount of carbon 14 in the cells of the plant or animal decreases.

For example, a living tree cell has five atoms of carbon 14. Ten thousand years after the tree is dead, only two atoms of carbon 14 are left. Twenty thousand years later only one atom of carbon 14 is left.

Knowing the number of carbon 14 atoms in a substance makes it possible to estimate the age of the substance. In recent years other radioactive elements with longer decay times are used for dating fossils.

HOMO HABILIS

Homo habilis is the oldest humanlike creature known. It lived about two million years ago. In 1964 a scientist named Louis Leakey found bones of *Homo habilis* in Olduvai Gorge in Africa. Its

Olduvai Gorge

Louis Leakey (left) holds the fossil remains he discovered in Olduvai Gorge. Today Leakey's fossils are part of the collection at the National Museum in Nairobi, Kenya (right).

brain size was worked out from the size of the skull bones. The brain was less than half the size of that of modern humans.

The bones of *Homo habilis* were small and delicate. Leakey named the creature *Homo habilis*, or "handy man," because stone tools were found near the skull. It appeared that this humanlike creature was skillful enough to use tools.

Homo habilis may have evolved (slowly changed and developed) over many years. Then a more advanced species appeared with a larger brain, thicker skull, heavy eyebrow ridges, and different teeth.

HOMO ERECTUS

Homo erectus, meaning "upright man," first appeared about 1.5 million years ago.

In 1891 Eugène Dubois, a Dutch doctor, was searching for prehistoric

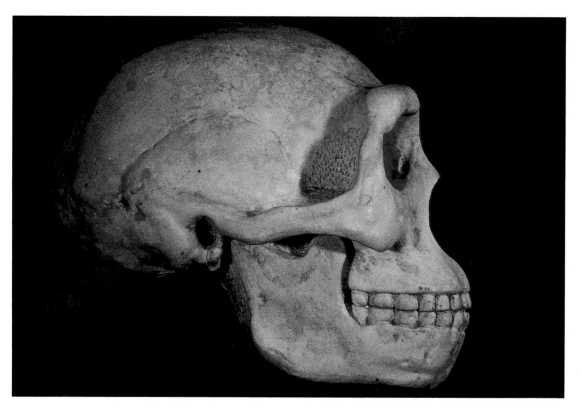

Cast made of the skull of *Homo erectus*

people. He found some apelike teeth and a skull in Java. The skull had a sloping forehead and heavy eyebrow ridges. The creature's brain was found

21

to be between the size of an ape's and a human's. About a year later, a thighbone was found near the same place. The shape of the bone suggested that the creature stood upright. Dubois called the skeleton the erect ape-man, or Java man.

Exhibit at the Field Museum in Chicago
recreates the world *Homo erectus* inhabited.

In 1900 an old tooth was dug up in a cave near a small town called Choukoutien near Peking, the capital of China. The tooth was studied carefully. It resembled the teeth of both apes and humans. In 1929 skulls and more bones were found in the Choukoutien cave. Scientists decided that these were the bones of a special group of prehistoric people. These

Model of the head of Peking man

people were given the
name Peking man.

Java man and Peking
man were similar because
they were like both apes
and humans. Today
scientists believe that the

Map shows where fossils of *Homo habilis* and *Homo erectus* have been found.

Heidelberg

EUROPE

ASIA

Beijing

AFRICA

Lake Turkana

Java

AUSTRALIA

two finds were examples
of the same species—
Homo erectus.

Homo erectus fossils
have been found in
Indonesia, China, Europe,
and Africa. Evidence has
been found that shows
that *Homo erectus* used
fire and lived in caves.

26

HOMO SAPIENS

More than 150,000 years ago, more advanced humans developed. They are called *Homo sapiens*. In 1857 some old bones were found in the Neanderthal Valley in Germany. Like those of *Homo erectus*, the bones looked both ape and human. The skull had a low forehead, thick bony eyebrows, large teeth, and a big lower jaw. Later,

Tools believed to have been used by Neanderthal man.

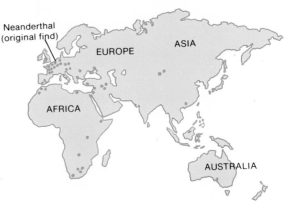

Map shows were fossils of *Homo sapiens* have been found.

similar skeletons were found. Scientists called the group Neanderthal man.

Neanderthals used spears and traps to hunt animals. Remains of Neanderthal man have been found all over the world. They are the oldest form of *Homo sapiens*.

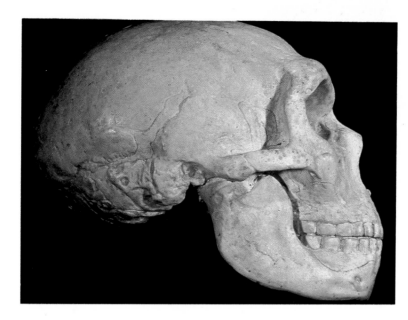

Cast made of
the skull of
Neanderthal man.

In 1868 some workers
found skeletons of five
human beings in a cave
called Cro-Magnon in
France. The skeletons
turned out to be at least
fifty thousand years old.
Scientists named this
group Cro-Magnon man.

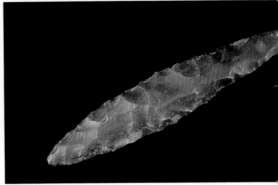

Exhibit at the Field Museum in Chicago (left) shows Cro-Magnon man. Scientists have found tools and weapons, such as the knife (below right), that were made by Cro-Magnon people.

The skeletons of Cro-Magnon man were very similar to the bones of humans today. Remains of Cro-Magnon people were found in North Africa, Asia, and Europe.

Cro-Magnons were the first to make tools from chipped stones and fishhooks and needles from bone, antler, and ivory.

Cro-Magnons were also great artists. They carved statues out of ivory and bone. They molded figures out of clay. They painted hunters and animals in bright colors on their cave walls. Scientists think that Cro-Magnons believed that

Bison painting (above) in Altimira Caves in Spain. Exhibit at the Field
Museum in Chicago (opposite page) shows Cro-Magnon man painting on a cave wall.

drawing an animal gave
them a magic power
over it. Cro-Magnons
may have believed that
this power would help
them find the animal and
kill it in the hunt.

HOW THE SPECIES WERE RELATED

Different species of these prehistoric people lived at different times. Their fossils were uncovered in different parts of the earth. How can this be explained?

In 1859 the English naturalist Charles Darwin wrote a book called *On the Origin of Species*. In it he explained how species

Charles Darwin
(1809-1883) wrote
On the Origin of Species.

developed, why they are
different, and how they are
related.

Darwin said that species
changed slowly with time.
New species developed, or
evolved, little by little out
of older species.

Scientists guess that *Homo habilis* may have changed slowly to become *Homo erectus*. *Homo erectus* then may have slowly evolved into *Homo sapiens*.

How do scientists explain species before *Homo habilis*? They cannot yet. Those early species are often called the missing links. Unless

Archaeologists work at the Grasshopper Site in Arizona.

scientists can find a
complete fossil record of
all prehistoric people, they
can only guess at how the
species might have
changed.

Scientists study pottery remains carefully looking for information about prehistoric people.

LEARNING FROM PREHISTORIC PEOPLE

Scientists study prehistoric people for many reasons. They want to find out what these people were like. How had they lived? Were they wanderers, hunters, or farmers? How did these people change over millions of years?

We know that the Cro-Magnons sewed. Scientists have found bone needles among the Cro-Magnon bones. From this simple tool we can guess that these early people sewed animal skins together to make clothes. However, were the bone needles used by women, or men? How did early people divide the work among themselves? Such information could help us to understand later human societies.

Some people think we inherit our behavior from our ancestors. Food sharing is one example. Like the Neanderthals and Cro-Magnons, we share our food and homes with our families. Prehistoric

Petroglyphs (rock carvings) on "Newspaper Rock" in Canyonlands, Utah record the hunting activities of an ancient people.

hunters brought food back to share with the people at home. Scientists know this because they found animal bones in the homes.

Exhibit at the Field Museum in Chicago represents the life of a prehistoric community that lived along the Wabash River in Illinois about 2500 B.C.

Prehistoric people were
hunters and gatherers.
They had to be physically
active in order to survive.
They chased after animals,
climbed trees, and moved

about gathering fruits and other things they needed.

People today no longer depend upon hunting. However, our bodies are very much like those of our ancestors. But we do not use them in the same ways. Today, in order to survive, we generally use our minds more than we do our bodies.

Above left: Alan Walker (left) and Richard Leakey, director of the National Museums of Kenya, study a *Homo erectus* skull found with the bones of an almost complete skeleton on the west side of Kenya's Lake Turkana.

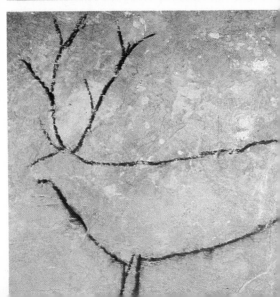

Stone Age tools from South Africa (above left), cave paintings from the Kangaroo Cave in Australia (top right), petroglyphs from Dinosaur National Park in Utah (middle right), and a drawing of a stag from Altimira Caves in Spain (right) give scientists information about life in prehistoric times.

By learning about
prehistoric people, we can
learn more about ourselves.
We can learn about our
families, our governments,
and our organizations.
We can learn about our
bodies and why they look
and work the way they do.
By finding out where we came
from, we can begin to understand
where we are going.

WORDS YOU SHOULD KNOW

ancestor(AN • sess • ter)—member of one's family line, such as a grandparent and those of earlier generations

behavior(bih • HAY • vyer)—the way a person acts and controls oneself

botanist(BAHT • ah • nist)—a specialist in the study of plant life

brain cells(BRAYN SELS)—neurons; nerve centers in the brain that control body movement

carbon dating(CAR • bun DAY • ting)—a system for tracing the age of matter, using the radioactive atom carbon 14

characteristics(kair • ik • ter • RISS • tix)—a person's identifying features, traits, gestures

decay(dih • KAY)—gradual disintegration; to rot, decompose

evolve(ee • VAHLV)—to expand, develop

flexible(FLEX • ih • bil)—easily movable; able to be bent, twisted

fossil(FAWSS • il)—petrified plant or animal remains dug from the earth

genus(GEE • nus)—animal or plant group having one or more characteristics, ranking above the species; name, capitalized, before species name, as *Homo sapiens*

Homo erectus(HO • mo ih • REK • tiss)—Latin name for species of first upright man, living about 1.5 million years ago

Homo habilis(HO • mo ha • BEEL • iss)—Latin name for the oldest humanlike creature known—two million years

Homo sapiens(HO • mo SAY • pee • enz)—Latin name for intelligent man; name of genus Man; species, intelligent; mankind

inherit(in • HAIR • it)—to receive from parents or ancestors, as traits, features

intelligence(in • TEL • ih • jence)—ability to understand, learn, reason

naturalist(NAT • choor • il • ist) — one who specializes in natural history, studies of plants and animals

prehistoric(pree • hiss • TOR • ik) — referring to time before history was written

radioactive(ray • dee • oh • ACK • tiv) — refers to ability of the atom of certain elements to send out special types of radiation at a definite rate of speed as it disintegrates, each element having a fixed "lifetime"

society(suh • SYE • ih • tee) — a community of persons having mutual interests or culture

species(SPEE • sees) — major subdivision of a genus, being the second of the scientific names classifying plants or animals having common characteristics but differing from other groups in the same genus

survival(ser • VIVE • il) — living beyond expected life span, especially through unusual or dangerous circumstances

INDEX

About the author

Ovid K. Wong earned his B.Sc. degree in biology from the University of Alberta, Edmonton, Canada, his M.Ed. in curriculum from the University of Washington, Seattle, and his Ph.D. in science education from the University of Illinois, Urbana-Champaign. He is currently the curriculum specialist for science, health, and outdoor education with school district #65 in Evanston. Since 1984 he has served as a consultant for the Illinois State Board of Education and the State Board of Higher Education. He also taught science at the center for Talent Development, Northwestern University. In 1987, Dr. Wong was appointed to serve on the Board of Directors, Chicago Heart Association and to chair the Science Advisory Committee, Educational Services Center of North Cook County.

Dr. Wong's work has appeared on public television and in such journals as Science Teacher, American Biology Teacher, ISTA Spectrum, The Bilingual Journal, *and a number of professional newsletters. Dr. Wong is the author of* A Glossary of Biology, Your Body and How It Works, Giant Pandas, Prehistoric People, *and* Experiments in Animal Behavior.